OPUS

25 YEARS OF HIS SUNDAY BEST

Berkeley Breathed

Little, Brown and Company
New York   Boston

To Jody, Sophie, and Milo

Also by Berkeley Breathed
Flawed Dogs
Edwurd Fudwupper Fibbed Big
The Last Basselope
Red Ranger Came Calling
Goodnight Opus
A Wish for Wings That Work

Little, Brown and Company
Time Warner Book Group
1271 Avenue of the Americas, New York, NY 10020
Visit our Web site at www.twbookmark.com

First Edition

ISBN 0-316-15994-8
Library of Congress Control Number 2004103826

10 9 8 7 6 5 4 3 2 1

LB

Printed in the United States of America

IN THE BEGINNING

I submit this primordial 1981 *Bloom County* Sunday panel as a candidate for my Big Twilight Zone Destiny-Messing Moment.

You'll note that it features a little blond-haired boy with an over-tweaked imagination working out his real-life anxieties and passions via space hero fantasies. Now *that's* a ripping Good Idea to build a classic comic strip around!

So naturally I only drew this one panel.

Most new comic strips don't survive such epic blunders. And *Bloom County* may well have headed for oblivion if in the following week I hadn't also drawn a mumbling penguin sitting on an ottoman watching TV. Mister Rogers asked his viewing tykes if they could say the word "tuba player" and Opus replied, "tuphlem grdlphump," and Mister Rogers said, "Good!" In 1981, this somehow was very funny. (And Michael Jackson was *not* — yet. A savage, backward era.)

So there it is: *a bird* was my Other Good Idea. More odd than good, really. This one almost slipped by too, but the fans — infinitely wise if not patient — let me know immediately. Opus stayed on his ottoman.

Five years later Bill Watterson's Calvin, aka Spaceman Biff, rocketed gloriously into America's Funny Papers, which was just how the comic universe was meant to be. Yet I came close to preempting Watterson with what surely would have become dreary space adventures of Milo battling Dukakis and Donald Trump aliens.

Like a toddler who imagines bouncing his ball into a freeway, I secretly love contemplating this pop culture pileup.

Two decades and 784 Sunday panels later, Opus still waddles among us. I built this retrospective collection around my favorite Sunday panels simply because they're the most fun. It's an immense pleasure to see them reproduced clear and sizable for once.

It's been a long, strange trip for this complicated penguin. Thanks for being along for the continuing ride.

Director Tim McCanlies called me in 2003 and described a movie called *Secondhand Lions* that he'd written and was presently filming in Texas about an adolescent boy — played by Haley Joel Osment — going to live with two crazy uncles, played by Michael Caine and Robert Duvall. At the end, the boy has become a cartoonist (where all coming-of-age movies should go), and his comic strip, *Walter and Jasmine,* stars the characters from his past.

Tim asked if I would draw the cartoon art that was to be hanging around the walls of the set. It'd been years since I'd sat at my cartooning table, so I thought it might be fun to invent a wholly fraudulent comic strip.

The film was terrific and I heard from a surprising number of people who recognized my hand in the art. Why is it here? Because if I hadn't had so much fun drawing these fake comics, it would never have occurred to me soon afterward that I should be drawing the real thing again. Life imitating art, as it should be.

BLOOM COUNTY

It's teeth-clenchingly obvious, but I'd like to point out the dramatic evolution of Opus from his first appearance to his present-day incarnation. Both in physical form and personality, he's been relentlessly evolving. I'm not sure that the Opus of today would recognize his scrawny 1981 version there on the left. Inversely, I suspect the early Opus would have an hysterical fit if he were to see where his nose ends up.

I've had nothing to do with this. At least not my conscious self.

This relentless march of Darwinian adaptation isn't necessarily a virtue for a comic strip. Readers seem to view changes in their favorite strips as they would changes in their plumbing: discomforting. But in my case, swinging wildly for the next creative hill is as natural (and irresistible) as breakdancing with my four-year-old in a Denny's. People around me squirm but I'm helpless to do anything about it.

As I'm intensely private, I resent that the only way I seem to be able to do this job is to make the writing personal. I'm scattered transparently throughout these characters. On a certain level, I'd be less embarrassed if I did a strip like *Marmaduke,* where people could only make conjectures about my dog's personal life rather than mine.

But alas, since life isn't standing still for me, I fear it won't for a small penguin.

All of which is to say that as in life, things change in my cartoons.

Kids:
Too much TV can
be super bad for
your eyes.

COME, STARTROOPER OPUS! WE HAVE PLANETS TO CONQUER AND AMAZON MARS BABES TO KIBITZ WITH..!!

CAN'T WAIT!

HELLO, RONALD-ANN. ANYTHING WRONG?

POOR REYNELDA DOESN'T MAKE A VERY GOOD TEA-PARTY GUEST.

WHAT HAPPENED?

SHE GOT CAUGHT IN THE CROSS FIRE DURING THE CHRISTMAS DRUG-TURF BATTLES...

BLEW HER LITTLE NOGGIN CLEAN OFF.

I SUUUUURE DO WISH SOMEONE WOULD COME TO MY TEA PARTY...

...WHO HAS A NOGGIN!

THE AMAZON MARS BABES ARE GETTIN' LONELY.

TEA'S GETTIN' COLD.

SIGH

A HEAD IS A TERRIBLE THING TO WASTE.

FOURTHS?

OUTLAND

I seem to be the author of a series of Ignominious Firsts in cartooning.

I was the first to quit a perfectly good and embarrassingly profitable comic strip. I was also the first to return with another comic after canceling the original, which had nothing wrong with it in the first place. I was also the first to do a strip only once a week. Then retire that one and declare that I was done with stripping once and for all.

Only to return eight years later and start all over again.

Warning to the impressionable young cartoonists watching: Don't try this stunt at home. Study Jim Davis's career instead.

As its inventor, I really don't know what to call a once-a-week cartoon panel. It's not really a comic strip in the traditional sense. It's something else . . . and something less, I fear. Showing up in their homes only on Sundays isn't as ingratiating to the readers as sharing coffee with them seven mornings a week. A Sunday-only strip simply cannot tell the stories nor instill the weirdly intimate familiarity readers can have with cartoon characters in a daily panel.

But what it *can* do is allow its author to keep from burning out and disappearing entirely. You've noticed that this has happened. A writing and drawing staff can forestall such an unfortunate scenario, but there's a creative price to be paid, I think.

So I scale back and take a few more naps. This, if little else, I share with G. W. Bush Jr.

SQUEEK SQUEEK...

MENTAL FLOSS

WAXED

OPUS

I stopped *Outland* because I wanted to learn to paint. Specifically, I wanted to learn how to tell a story through paintings. I authored six picture books.

After the paint was dry on the last one — *Flawed Dogs* — I looked again at the comic strip world. There had been a technological revolution in the eight years I'd been gone: the Internet — God bless those dear Google Boys — eliminated the desperate, last-minute searches at faraway libraries for a picture of, say, a Segway scooter or what an elephant looks like from the rear when it squats — legs out or under?

Photoshop had given us the power to color our own comics and come darn close to painting them. Imagine: actually something that *looks* cool on a comic page. Unthinkable in 1990.

And chasing Fed Ex trucks in the wee hours of the morning was no more. Broadband was a permanent deliverance from that resident evil.

What ex mobster/cartoonist could resist such provocation? *"Just when I thought I was out . . . they PULL me back in!"*

And they did. I wanted to get to know Opus better and see him better defined.

And I wanted to draw. An increase in square inches and technology had allowed this. You can see that in the new strips. See something else: I'm enjoying myself. I hope that you can picture me with a stupid, goofy grin as I draw some of this stuff. Trust me: many cartoonists have long since stopped amusing themselves.

A pity.